Uncharted
Existence.

Christabelle Marbun

"If I read a book and it makes my whole
body so cold no fire can ever warm me,
I know that is poetry"
-Emily Dickinson

*Dedicated to the Sunny days in May,
knowledgeable fools in unexplored
Alleyways, getting lost in the Savannah,
and the Matters of Victories.*

Christabelle Marbun

*To the world I have fallen
madly in love with.*

Plethora

pleth·o·ra

/ˈpleTHərə/

Learn to pronounce

noun
1. 1.
    So much of everything.

Christabelle Marbun

So I will dim the world just a little,
In order to hear you speak.

I had been walking around aimlessly
for far too long now.
But in those long walks, I have managed
to find something I didn't know I was
searching for.

And was it worth it?
Did you find infinity,
or instead endless mortality?

I hope you frame the loss
and cherish the hurt.
For the victories do not need
to outshine what truly makes you.

Her.

So she found it, the very meaning to the night sky she loved so much. She hardly hopes and hopes to hurt. The night sky was nothing more than just that, but to her, it meant teaching herself to see in the dark again. In every star she saw the times she fought and in every particle of dark matter she saw the times she lost. She lived like she wanted no tomorrow, she loved like no one had seen, and she hoped that one day the world would pick her out of the bunch and show her the secrets of the stars. She wanted to be loved as much as she did the moon, she wanted someone to see her the way she does dark matter, and she wanted for someone to find the very meaning of who they are in her like she does the night sky. She was a stranger to the ground she laid on, her eyes were of sunsets eager to touch the stars. She had found it, right there, right here.

The very meaning of the night sky she loved so much.

I'm often glad that it's nothing, because
to me, nothing is the absence of the
terrifying something.

I don't need you to die for me,
I need you to live for me.
Because the hard part is living.

"There can never be a mind like yours every century,

Death said,

"The power and pain are far too great a price."

I knew I would lose it.
I knew one day it will all be gone.
So before that happens,
I will teach you how to love,
I will show you how I live,
And I will write you the unexplainable.
I will teach you how to say goodbye.

There are so many things I would like to tell you, so many paragraphs I haven't written, but right now, silence is all I have to offer.

It hurt to look at you,
It hurt to watch you make me
Promises you cannot keep.

I long for the day my eyes will no longer
be foreign to me.

Lavenders had always reminded her how
simple beauty can be.

Don't remind me of the things
that make you warm,
I don't need to start missing
something I don't know.

The ink stained her,
She had never known what it truly
felt like to be hurt by her own pen.

It broke me to hurt you,
But it broke you if I stayed.

Do you see it now?
It's not the race that kills you,
It's the finish line that's the end.
Because the fall is fleeting,
It's the stop that's far more deadly.

Breathe,
It's okay.
Let your lungs
Love the blue skies.

If I could tell my heart anything,
It would be a thank you.
Thank you for giving so much,
And never asking for anything in return.

The words started to appear on the walls, haunting her and reminding her of a gift she wished she didn't have.

You are every wonderful story,
Every painful metaphor,
And all the brightest colors,
Put together, all at once,
and released into the world.

"My darling,

Death gently said,

"You must live as if the stars had created
you themselves."

So I'm sorry I'm a lot,
I'm sorry I'm exhausting.
It's just that- I know, trust me,
I have to live with myself.
But of course, the plethora of voices this
world pours out will always be there, and
I'm sorry you will too.
And I will try to quiet it all,
Even when you tell me not to.

For it is in the unfinished pages where the greatest stories lie.

Do not lie to yourself in order to achieve
false happiness,
It will only damage your chance at the pure
joy you truly deserve.

The End of the World

She was clothed in the art she made,
She spoke with poisonous elegance,
And seized with unparalleled love.
She was every art movement,
Every scientific consensus,
And every disprovable theory.
She was the beauty of
The harsh world,
The kind that would end it.

I had to ask myself every day,

"Did you really run off
to find yourself,

Or were you running away from who you
are because you were terrified of what you
could become?"

Don't Forget You're Human

I hope you lived,
I hope you didn't cower in your comfortable
bubble of pain.
But I also hope you did not live so infinitely
that you forgot what it felt like to get hurt
and be mortal.

Everything?

There is so much of everything,
I don't know how to tell you there is.
But I want it all, I want to take it all.
I want to breathe the everything in even if I
don't have the capacity for it.
So give me the dark nights, give me the
papercuts, give me the sunsets, give me the
laughter, and give me the kind of pain that
paralyzes you. Because I will feel it all, just
for the sake of experiencing my mortality in
the most infinite way I can.

She wanted to transcend every feeling of
pain she had ever felt, or rather, the
excessive amounts of it, onto paper.
She wished that for once she got to read her
story like a book, one that could never truly
harm her, but make her feel all the same.

And who are we to assume that the sun prefers to be the center of our universe?

Bad was never the enemy of Good,
I had learned that Perfection was.

You became everything I love about the world, the rainy days, hot nights, cold shoulders, and heated fights. You are every good and bad thing I could think of, every good and bad thing I have come to love. That amount of passion could not simply be released into the universe, so they gave me you. Someone to love as madly, wildly, and excessively as I do the rest of everything.

Glorified Words

"What even *is* poetry?"

"I like to think it is the act of appreciating something in its deepest form of beauty."

"And who might you be?"

Asked the White Rabbit,

"I'm the girl who is madly in love with a world that will never love her the same."

I had to teach myself slowly, step by step,
one sleepless night after the other, that the
world that gave me a reason to cry was also
the world that gave me the capacity to fall in
love with being human.

I was angry,
Angry at a world that gave me a curse but
taught me to love it as a miracle.

But at the end of the day, I wish not to say goodbye to the overwhelming.

Christabelle Marbun

Darkness

dark·ness

/ˈdärknəs/

Learn to pronounce

noun
noun: **darkness**; plural noun: **darknesses**
1. 1.
Something that is not always terrifying.

I would love to tell you that I stopped counting, that I spent fewer nights on the bathroom floor. But no, I stayed in the same place I've always been, waiting for the day when Better comes to me.

Walk with pain in your heart,
For it is then when you cannot take more.

Christabelle Marbun

After all those nights I spent in fear,
I can finally say,
You can find me in the Dark.

I've always been fond of sunsets,
In the way that I can't wait what happens
when it's dark.

<u>Su*c!de Note.</u>

The pen glides against the paper,
As if urging her to write her final words
just a little faster.

And there will be a time when the world will
let go of your hand and give you mine.

I kept crying, it hurt.
My chest burned and my eyes stung.
It was so overwhelming and just the thought
of it scared me. But after, after it all, I see
the wreckage, and I am reminded that the
ship needed to tear apart so that I will not
drift in the sea forever.

I'm sorry that I hurt and I'm sorry that I can't heal. I'm sorry I apologize too much and I'm sorry that I'm too determined to protect you from myself that I refused to let you in. It's just that right now, you're the best thing I have, and I could never forgive myself for hurting the best thing that has ever happened to me.

Just because the darkness and pain are familiar does not mean it is safe.

The Friendly Kind of Pain.

I will admit that I know nothing.
And it the midst of not knowing, I have
come to understand that the pain in the
unknown will make itself visible eventually.
The kind of pain that incapacitates you, the
one that chains you to your bed for days on
end without wanting to eat or drink. And
when that kind of pain arrives, I know I
must welcome it, tell it to make itself
comfortable, and when it leaves, tell it to
leave the door open behind it. Because
whether what comes next is pain or love,
I am ready to accept it. For what else are we
to do when we know nothing?

The thoughts will always be there,
The temptation of that release
will always be there.
But just because the darkness is here to stay,
Doesn't mean you get to find a million
reasons not to.

I'm not asking you to fight,
I'm asking you to breathe.
Because although fighting
may be more satisfying,
Breathing is just as hard.

Christabelle Marbun

She was eloquent in her poison,
    And ethereal with her kills.

Have you ever seen it?
A pair of eyes that seem to carry it all.

Have you ever seen a pair of eyes that still
show glimpses of the light that has been
sucked out of them?

I hope you never forget, that just how a
lightning bolt may look like growing roots,

Pain can often feel like security.

I hated it.
I hated you.
You made me wish the world would
disappear with you along with it.
But you had the nerve to hold my hand
through the hurricane, you had the audacity
to hold me when I refused you, and I hated
you for loving me more than I did myself.

It is a painful revelation,
To know that it often takes Death
to teach us the most valuable lessons of Life.

A Bottle of Pills.

She was the kind to fidget with
life and death between her fingers.
The familiar rattle of her memories
echoed in the dark.
She toyed with the idea of letting the small
bottle take her. She twirled it between her
fingers, as the control she has over it gave
her an unmatched euphoria.

"Why?" Some might ask.

Because she knows she cannot convince
herself to wake up tomorrow morning.

I met them when I was just a young girl,
They stood in front of me,
extending their hand.

"Hello,

They spoke.

I'm Darkness,"

"And I will be your dearest friend."

Your bravery is incredible.

How do I know this?
Because you wake up every day
And walk past the blade and bottle of pills
knowing that it is a ticket out,
But never taking it.

I'm afraid I have taught myself to trust my
imagination more than I do the truth.

"Child, are you lost?"
Death asked,

"I ran away,
Said the little girl.

I don't like Life very much, he's quite
unkind. I would like to stay here."
Death smiled,

"My dear girl, you must be kind to
Life even when he is not to you. It is
unfair, but it is worth it."
The little girl frowned.

"When may I come back here?"
Death gently picked her up,

"My good friend, Time, will take you
here someday. Now come, we must
take you home."

Oh, to live in a world where
hurting is not the default,
And the sickly-sweet lies
are not systemic.

I am fortunate enough to say that growing up has taught me that eventually, the Darkness will be my hero.

The light became blinding,
So I ran.
I took refuge in the dark,
And discovered the wonderous unknown.

Uncharted Existence

There was nothing but silence,
Life had led me into the Dark Room
and shut the door behind it.
The quiet became a symphony that
became far more familiar than my own
heartbeat.

Just then, after the orchestra has played
their final note of silence, I hear the sizzling
sounds of a match in the distance. Freshly
struck, inviting me in. Death was waiting for
me there, leading me towards the door.

She turned the handle and the door swung
open, I looked up at Her and she smiled.

"You see? The door was never locked. You
are always welcome here, but take it from
me, Life is not as selfish as you believe."

And the next time I saw Her, she opened
Her door to me like an old friend.

Christabelle Marbun

I stay up late,
Sometimes all night,
Trying to piece
together the world,
Only to take it all apart,
and hoping to call it art.

Do not spend your days searching for
someone when you don't know who you are,
Trust me, it is not worth losing what you
thought you knew.

Christabelle Marbun

It's not that I am afraid of
losing myself here,
I simply fear that I am
Finding myself in the dark.

How many more do you suppose you will write? What more variations of combined words will it take for you to finally see that your love for darkness will destroy you?

Christabelle Marbun

I never blamed the Dark for the
absence of my childhood.
For it was the Light that
stole it from me.

Sometimes a fuse would happen and the power in my room would go out for just a second. When I was younger, I would scream
and run towards the door.
I am 16 years old now, a fuse happens and the power in my room goes out for just a second.
I feel the urge to scream, but nothing comes. I do not rush to light a candle, my eyes do not desperately search for the doorway, and in my moment of panic, I had learned to enjoy the company of the dark.

Oh to be alive in a world
where death was worshipped.

So do not wait.
Do not wait for the lemons
to be handed to you.
Learn to nourish the tree
you have sown yourself.

Christabelle Marbun

I tried to feel my way through,
Stretching out my hands hoping
someone would find me.
And when no one did,
I learned to hold my own,
And danced through the darkness.

"Take care of her,"
Life said gently.

"Of course my dear,
I always do."
Death smiled.

Life gave a sad smile.

"I'm sorry I won this time."
Said Death,

"It's all right,

Life smiled,

I don't mind losing to you my love."

Christabelle Marbun

Thank you for staying,
Even in the dark,
Thank you for staying.

The candle was burning out.
I gently shielded it from
the wind with my hand.
Without it I won't know
where I'm going.
But as it faded away, I knew,
I had no choice but to
grow accustomed to the dark.

Please Stay.

Please still be here in the morning,
The midnights of the mind will end.
I cannot promise you light will return,
And I cannot promise you the days will get
better. But the world is here, and so are you.
Please still be here in the morning,
I cannot convince you to stay, only you can.

I will write you better days,
I will paint better nights,
I will be here forever if you need me to,
And I will hope to see you smile.
The blinding light will not be here forever,
And the darkness is not so terrifying.
I will write you better days,
And I will paint you better nights,
I will be here forever,
As long as you promise to fight.

You are everything you need
to guide yourself through the darkness.

Love

/ləv/

Learn to pronounce

See definitions in:
noun
    1.   1.

        The most irrational thing we can do, but we do anyway.

So she sat there,
Letting the tears run down her eyes.
Overwhelmed by the notion that
life had loved her for the very first time.

I will spend the rest of my life writing you
stars, painting you tears, and showing you
everything I love about you.

Do not tell me you love me.
That is a very dangerous thing to say
to someone who only knows how to love.

So did you fall in love with me instantly,
Or did you instantly know that you could
love me?

If you told me yesterday that
I would fall in love,
I would smile and kindly say,
"Love was never for me, but that's quite
alright. I have learned to admire it in others,
the glow in their eyes is truly a sight to see."

Uncharted Existence

You loved me, and I loved you,
But my pen didn't like us on paper.

Don't lie to me,
If you must leave, then you will.
I have learned to live even when love leaves.

The rest of the world knew,
I did too.
That you, my sweet sun,
could not love me forever.

My darling, I have never thought there would come a day when I would love someone almost as much as I did death.

No.
You don't get to beg me to stay.
That's not fair.
You do not get to tell me
that there's so much more to life.
You do not get to remind me
of the world I love so much.
You do not get to make me
want this again.
Please.

Don't make me want this again.

Somehow,
Love is the only thing humanity got right,
And still do wrong.

Love like it's your final days.
Hell, love like life is already over.

Love was not what I thought it would be,
It shifted, changed, hurt,
But for the first time,
Love was something
I don't mind running after.

You've tried everything,
And in a final desperate attempt you would
say to me,
      "Please?"
I'd turn to look at you, hoping my eyes
would explain it all. Because I don't want to
leave, I don't want to hurt you, but you will
hurt anyway if I stay.
You turn your back to me and you'd say,
      "Please"
As if turning your back would make it easier
for you to walk away.
I tried to search for your eyes, but yours
would never meet mine. Because you
wanted to know if I would stay for *you*, and
not just for your eyes.
You ask me one more time, this one with a
little less hope in it,
      "Please."
And for the first time in my life, I'd say,

    "Okay, just for a little while."

I didn't mean to,
I swear I didn't.
You were there to love me
but instead you became a casualty.
I'm sorry. God I'm so sorry.
You promised me everything,
But here we are,
You loving and me hoping.
Hoping you'd understand enough
To let me go.

You have to give yourself infinity,
And you must love like the rest of
the world has turned you down.

The stars will never know you
if they never meet your eyes,
The oceans will not hear your voice
if you never scream,
And the earth will not feel you
if you never cry.

I'm running out of things to tell you,
So please, don't leave.

Do not blame me for it,
For Life had hurt me again.
So do not blame me for running to Death.
Because Death showed me true love.

It just hit me today,
For the first time, I don't
love the idea of loving someone.
I love *you*,
And there's nothing
you can do about it.

For 16 Years

You taught me to forgive,
But it took me a while to realize,
That you taught me to forgive
over and over because you wanted me to
keep forgiving you over and over.
Even if it killed me.

I hope you know that you do not
have to fall into it now, that someday, one
day, some time, it can happen. And even if it
doesn't, know that you can always fall
madly for yourself.

I was truly hoping you'd change the ending,
Change it to something different.
Because at this point, I was tired of reading
the same final chapter over and over.

Don't you ever get tired of it?
Tired of knowing that you're
Making promises you can't keep?

I'm going to hurt you someday,
It's not an insecurity, it's a fact.
But with you I know that won't be the end.
Because we will fix it, we will do better,
And we will continue to choose each other.

You didn't love me,
You simply wanted someone
that needed to not be alone.

Little did you know,
That the top of the world
Was the passenger seat in your car.

Don't be afraid to break me,
For I am not fragile.
But be cautious in how you love me,
For it's the most poisonous of love
that can kill.

How do I do this?
Teach me how to accept
this kind of love when
my definition of it
has always been violence.

You raised me,
And I can never repay you.
You hurt me,
but for that I ask for
nothing in return.

(Bad) Parenting

Teach me how to unlearn
everything you've taught me,
Tell me how to untie the ropes
You taught me to weave,
And show me how to die
Better than I lived.

I ask myself every day,

Was I in love with you,

Or was I in love with the game?

Christabelle Marbun

I am terrified that to me,
Love means enjoying manipulating you.

Don't worry about losing them someday,
Yes, it can happen.
But for now,
As long as you wake up every day and
Choose to love each other,
You have everything you need.

Will it still be requital then?
Your love for me?

Will you still be here when
I am no longer broken?

I never asked much of you,
I never hoped to see you at Christmas.
And yet when I hear your footsteps down
the hall, I flinch just a little.

The definitive answer to infinity
is irrationality.
A substitute for this is love.

"Why, why me?

She said with eyes
full of tears.

It hurts. Did you know that? It hurts
so bad. And I never want to do it
again."

Life approached her slowly,

"My darling, when will you see it?"

He said lifting her chin.

"It is a gift to love like that."

Christabelle Marbun

I'm still here,
I'm still hoping.
Hoping that you will one day see
That I will not be here forever.

You don't always have to fight for it.
Those four-letter words.
They are there for you, and they can be
found elsewhere.
So when it starts to poison you,
Let them go.
Because those four-letter words,
Can always be found elsewhere.

Christabelle Marbun

Elanguescence

e·lan·gue·scence

Learn to pronounce

noun

1. (n) The soul's gradual loss of its powers.

2. The gradual process of fading away into non-existence

The ink will stain your hands,
They will mark them with all
The painted tragedies and
untold victories.
And by the end of it all,
There will be a story
you would want to tell.

I locked myself in,
Because I wanted to protect you
From who you thought I was.

Do not tell her to count the stars
like it's her last night,
do not tell her to live
like there's no tomorrow.
Because if it's her last night alive,
she would be spending it
teaching you how to let go.

Do not mistake
her kindness as happiness.
She is emptying her cup
so that it's easier to leave.

Échec et mat (Checkmate).

I meticulously moved the pieces one by one. Strategically looking for the moves that will not harm me, hoping that a catalyst will never arrive. The black and white squares are taunting me now, And you moved a simple pawn. I wasn't sure if that was a plan to kill or nothing at all. I see a window to attack, and perhaps even kill. But I looked at you, and your eyes told me the game isn't meant to be over, not yet. We kept moving them, placing them in corners we thought the other would never find. The pieces glided as we danced across the board, Wanting to take our time to the inevitable outcome.

Every time I hit the clock my heart rate rises, as if my whole body knew the brutal endgame was next. You moved that pawn again, then I saw it. The fatal move that could end this all. The music dimmed, time stopped, and my eyes froze. I sat there; eyes glued to your King. This was not what I wanted for us. I tried to meet your eyes, and they were filled with the kind of fear I knew all too well. Your eyes begged me to make the kill quick and painless. So I gently pick up my Queen and softly set it next to your King. We both knew, this was it. I watched as you gently laid your King down, the thud of the piece hitting the board was jarring. You got up and smiled, but before you left, you slipped the pawn into your pocket. I knew I would never play anyone like you ever again. Deep down I knew the cost was far too great. This time, the checkmate wasn't worth it.

You never truly valued her.
You just wanted to believe
you still had hope in humanity.
So you learned to love
the most hopeless one.

Stain her, leave your mark.
She'll fade away soon.
So with all due respect,
Do your worst.

To the rest of the world she was rare,
But to the stars, she was one of them.

I have come to learn that people
are simply made up of internal conflicts.
And over time, you can see
the gradual loss of the soul in them.

How foolish we are to be marveled by infinity. When we, as humans, have been trying to define *forever*

She has given so much of herself away,
That she doesn't have much of herself left.
So even the bad and the painful,
She now keeps near.

My greatest fear is that one day,
I might not miss the feeling of being human.

Try to find it,
In the relentless chapters
in that book of yours.
Try to find the soul
you once loved living with.

.

I now know why storms
are named after people.

Will you live with me?
Will you love me even
when I am fixed?
Will you come to understand
my fascination with death?
Because otherwise,
Do not hold me.
Do not show me addictive kindness.
Because you will incapacitate me,
I will be powerless,
And I will not have the strength to let go.

Perhaps I will remind you
how you have made it this far,
Your unparalleled sense of stubbornness
Has made you very difficult to kill.

How to: Take Care of a Universe.

The delicacy of her universe is such a finite thing. It's something that no one can ever get quite right. It's an art form that's easy for even her to get wrong. She often has no idea how to keep it in balance. When she loses control, she causes solar flares, when she is hurting the stars will burst, and when her heart is broken the suns will fall. But just like her pain, her euphoria's will do the same. Her laughter will cause meteor showers, her hopeful smiles will give shooting stars, and her love will create planets.

When taking care of a solar system, there are no instructions, no guidelines or directions as to how to nourish them. You must simply trust that they will know how to grow and always be there for them. You must understand that there will be bad days, but those days will not stay forever. One solar flare does not end a universe. You will always be there to catch her world in your hands, but you must also trust that dark matter will hold up her universe. It's a delicate art, taking care of her. But the love she gives you in return is undeniably infinite.

How much of me left do you want?
I have given you every part of me,
Even the worst. What more will you take?

Christabelle Marbun

.

I started losing days,
        Then you,
                Then me.

To look inward is to learn of your flaws,
And to me, when that happens, when I learn
which flaws to fix and which to love,
That is when life begins.

Perhaps you won't find a happy ending.
Perhaps you will stay right where you are.
But you forget, happy endings
are not places.
They are
people,
moments,
memories.
They are the painful days, sleepless nights,
wonderful laughter, and tears you shed for
all the right reasons.

My dear, happy endings are found
when you are truly content.

I have written all the poems,
Thought of all the stanzas.
I would like to return to a world,
Where I am allowed hurt in
a manner that isn't metaphorical.
A world where the pen
must not always meet paper,
and where love might not
always be found.

When the world has made their stance
against you clear, you learn to love a life
even if it has not been kind to you.

How many days have you gone without
breathing? You must leave it all behind.
Shut the door and walk away.
Leave
     The metaphors
              Be.
Let them stay hidden for now. I promise you
they will find you again.

"How does that make you feel?"

It doesn't.
"Hurt, I guess?"

You can never truly lose yourself.
Because even when you don't know who
you are, how you choose to find it tells you
exactly what you need to know.

I tried to shift in my bed
to make myself more comfortable,
Comfortable enough to say goodbye.
I held my breath trying to build up the
courage to tell you.
You said nothing,
And for a moment, I wish you did.
I wish you fought; I wish *I* fought.

But the fact that neither of us
Tried to stay said it all.

It broke me,
You were over the phone.
Your exhales begged me to stay.
I glanced at the bottle of pills on my
nightstand, and for a moment, I considered
staying. I was a child in the brightness,
blinded by the very thing that could kill me.
But here we are, and here I am.
Still believing that
I only come to the edge for the view.

I lost a lot of it,
The kind of hope that a child has.
I still miss it sometimes, having it.
But I have come to know that some things
were never meant for me to have.

You don't see it.
You don't see everything I've lost in the
battle to protect what I have left.
You don't know what's at stake.
And you don't get to tell me it will get
better.

Christabelle Marbun

She knows herself as a small ocean,
And she recognizes her love as vast as skies.

Uncharted Existence

You found my soul,
Built it, loved it, adjusted it into place.
You wrote your name on it, and it was mine.

When the soul has selected its infinity,
Then, my love, you need not worry of
finding your identity.

And all of your efforts,
For what have they been?
Were you truly trying to find yourself,
or did you go to great lengths only to hold
on to something you knew you lost
a long time ago?

I sat on a park bench that fit me perfectly,
There I watched many go by.
Life sat down next to me,

"It's been a long time, old friend"

I turn to look at Him and smiled,

"Indeed, it has."

Humans have always thought that Life and
Death are enemies, but little do they know,
that we were both once in love.

I ran to her,
The little girl hugging her knees
with her back against the door.
I scooped her up into my arms
as she cries,

      "I'm sorry. I'm so sorry."

She looks up at me,

      "Why are you sorry?"

I smiled guiltily,

      "Because I'm afraid
      I've disappointed us."

She wipes away her tears as she presses her
small hand on my heart,

      "It's still beating, and for that, I can
      never be disappointed."

How am I supposed to believe you will be
here for me when you have left others?

I hate you for making me hate the
only part of me I have taken so long
to learn to love.

It will hurt,
You will bleed,
It will be unbearable,
And you will scream.
But I promise you,
It will be worth it.
All the sleepless nights,
Ceiling views,
Empty hands,
And broken trusts.
Because one day
You will see,
That you are worth
So much more than infinity.

Uncharted Existence

;

Printed in Great Britain
by Amazon

61211485R00102